MACHINE LEARNING

FOR BEGINNERS

See more books:
https://www.auvapress.com/books

Leave a review on Amazon:

https://www.auvapress.com/amazon-review/machine-learning-beginners

MACHINE LEARNING

STEP BY STEP COMPREHENSIVE GUIDE SIMPLIFIED

FOR BEGINNERS

MATT GATES

AUVA PRESS

Trademarks:

Auva Press and the Auva Press logo are trademarks or registered trademarks and may not be used without written permission. All other trademarks are the property of their respective owners and use in an editorial fashion to the benefit of the trademark owner, with no intention of infringement of the trademark. Auva Press is not associated with any product or vendor mentioned in this book.

FIRST EDITION

ISBN-13: 978-1-5470-3904-3
ISBN-10: 1-5470-3904-3

Editor: Audrey Swans
Cover Designer: Howard West

To my dearest and family,
your support have been the great source of strength
and making this possible

CONTENTS

PREFACE

Machine learning has become the pillar of information technology (IT), albeit hidden over the past few years. Today, we are surrounded by several machine learning–based technologies across a broad spectrum of applications, such as credit card–fraud detection systems, software systems that filter out spam messages, and search engines that are always learning to bring us better results.

Unlike conventional programs, machine-learning programs utilize humanlike artificial intelligence (AI) to learn from experience rather than just follow explicit instructions, which enables these programs to adapt on their own and detect more complex data patterns during the computational process. This is not possible through conventional programing techniques. As ever-expanding volumes of data are collected, "smart" data analysis will become ubiquitous and an integral component of any technological system.

In the following chapters, you will learn all the ins and outs of machine learning over a wide range of applications, exploring some of the basic tools from statistics and probability theory that define how machine-language problems are framed and understand fairly basic yet effective algorithms that solve complex machine-learning problems. Let's jump in.

Chapter 1

Introduction To Machine Learning

In machine learning, also known as automated learning, computers are programed to learn from any input that they are given and provide answers to complex problems. The input for any learning process or algorithm is the training data, which represents the experience, while the output is some complex task performed by a software program.

But more specifically, the biggest query that should concern us at this stage is "How do we represent the training data or input so that experience can be described?"

And how can the process of automated learning be achieved in programs? In this chapter, we delve deeper into these concepts of machine learning to give you a general idea of machine learning.

Let's dive in.

What is learning?

Learning can be described as any process that converts experience into knowledge or expertise. Let me explain using a couple of examples.

For example, when mice come across an unfamiliar food that looks or smells good, they eat it in small quantities at first. If the food tastes bad or makes them sick, the mice associate that food with illness and consequently avoid it from then on. Likewise, this behavior can be found in other animals in the wild when venturing into new territories.

On the other hand, if the food doesn't have any ill effects on their bodies, the mice continue eating the food. Obviously, a learning process has taken place: the mice have used their experience eating the food to acquire basic knowledge of the safety of that food, automatically predicting that it will have the same effect on their bodies when encountered in the future.

Another example of learning is training dogs to do an action like rolling on the ground or simply sit and await instruction. Every action or task completed successfully is rewarded with food. This reinforces the learning process of the dog through repetition training. The dog learned that food will rewarded for task been done correctly upon instruction and will follow this instruction even if there are no presence of food.

Let us now examine a typical machine-learning process. Suppose you would like to program a computer to learn how to filter out spam e-mails. A simple solution would resemble the learning process that mice use to avoid poisonous foods: you would just program the computer to identify, categorize and memorize all the e-mails that the user labeled as spam, then search for identical e-mails among the new ones.

If a new e-mail matched one on the spam list, it would automatically be labeled as such and trashed. Otherwise, it would be stored in the user's inbox.

While the process of learning by memorization is sometimes worthwhile, it lacks an integral component of any efficient learning process—inductive reasoning, the ability to learn broad generalizations from specific examples. In other words, it would be better to program the computer to learn how to discern the types of e-mail messages that the user considers to be spam. To achieve such generalization in the spam-filtering process, the program could scan the known spam e-mails and mine a set of words that often appear in spam messages. By checking new e-mails for these suspicious words, the program could then correctly predict whether an unfamiliar e-mail message would be labelled as spam.

However, inductive reasoning shouldn't be the only approach that machine-learning systems use.

What will distinguish learning mechanisms in spam filtering program that just result in new emails being labeled as spam or stored in the box from useful learning process?

Answering this question is vital to the development of machine learning systems. While people can depend on common sense to filter out the random spam messages, computers don't have common sense.

Therefore, so we must define refined principles that protect the programs need refined principles to prevent them from reaching illogical and meaningless conclusions. The development of these principles is what underpinnings of machine learning–program design.

To summarize, prior experience combined with principles biasing the learning task is the key to creating a successful learning process. Therefore, every well-designed machine-learning system requires tools that express a domain expertise, translate this expertise into a learning bias, and quantify the bias's effect on the success of learning.

When is machine learning important?

Under what circumstances do you need a machine-learning system rather than a conventional program that ordinary computers can handle? There are two types of problems that machine learning can solve:

- Tasks that are too complex to be programed
- Need for adaptively generated tasks

Let's explore these circumstances.

1. Tasks that are too complex to be programed

For various reasons, not all tasks can be described using conventional programing languages; some tasks are too complex in their requirements or lack clarity in defining the application interface. We can group these tasks into two sets:

- ***Tasks that are routinely performed by people and animals.*** There are several tasks, such as driving, speech recognition, and image recognition, that we perform regularly in everyday life and yet cannot describe sufficiently enough to create a conventional program. In all these tasks, programs have to learn from experience to achieve satisfactory output, which requires machine-learning systems.

- ***Tasks that are beyond human capabilities***. These tasks involve complex analysis to turn large sets of data into useful information for decision-making. For instance, medical-archive data, weather-prediction data, genomic data, and search engines are all too large and unstructured for conventional SQL to process. But as more and more data are digitally recorded, it is becoming increasingly evident that a treasure-trove of meaningful information is buried in these databases, and the only way to find it is by developing machine-learning systems to help mine the data. If you would like to know more about data analytics and mining, the previous book in this series, *Data Analytics for Beginners*, discusses these topics in greater detail.

2. Need for adaptively generated tasks

One of the limitations of conventional programs is their rigidity; once these programs are coded, tested, and installed, they remain unchanged, performing the same tasks over and over again. But numerous tasks vary from user to user, and machine-learning programs are better equipped to perform these tasks, since they can adapt their behavior to different contexts and environments. Typical examples of such programs include:

- Programs that decode handwritten text, easily adapting to the various handwriting styles of different users
- Spam-detection programs that adapt automatically to any changes in spam e-mails
- Speech-recognition programs that readily adapt to the various speech patterns of different users

Applications of machine learning

Machine learning is a fantastic revolution in AI. Today, both cutting-edge startups and established firms are finding more and more ways to utilize machine learning in their business operations. Here are some examples of machine-learning applications to various fields:

#1: Finance

In the financial world, online learning and decision-making take place in a wide variety of scenarios that can change depending on the business environment, the available feedback, and the nature of the decision. These decisions can involve stock trading, ad placement, route planning, or even picking a heuristic move.

The machine-learning algorithms that are used in online stock trading ensure the best possible outcomes in two ways. First, they help prevent stockholders from making the worst trades. Second, their benchmark principles narrow down decisions to the most profitable strategies.

Machine learning can also help banks discover important new insights in data, enabling them to compete better and increase their bottom lines. Such data mining assists not only in determining the best investment opportunities but also in identifying high-risk customer profiles and detecting signs of fraud.

#2: Big Data and Analysis

Today, data scientists are having a lot of problems efficiently storing the vast amounts of data in their organizations, let alone learning anything from them. Data collection has been growing exponentially at a rate of over 45 percent every year, and an astonishingly large portion of this growth is stemming from either unstructured or semi-structured data that can't be handled by the conventional relational database-management systems.

Managing such data requires a disruptive approach, and machine learning hasn't disappointed in this regard. From medical fields to retail stores to election-campaign management, machine learning is helping organizations derive new insights from data, which they then use to tailor their services to their clients' behavioral patterns.

For instance, online storefronts are now using machine learning to recommend items that you may like based on analysis of your purchasing history. Similarly, machine learning has enabled the healthcare industry to develop wearable devices and sensors that use large volumes of data to assess patients' health in real time, reducing readmission rates at hospitals and helping healthcare professionals improve their diagnoses.

#3: Statistical research

Machine Learning has become the pillar of IT, albeit hidden over the past few years. From search engines that are constantly learning to bring us the best results to anti-spam software systems that filter out spam messages to credit card fraud detection systems, the list of machine learning applications is endless.

One universal trait of these applications is the complexity of data patterns that should be analyzed during the computational process. The conventional programming techniques are inadequate because they don't provide explicit and refined user requirements that specify how the tasks should be computed. In particular, machine-learning applications should utilize intelligence such as that possessed by human beings to learn from experience rather than just following explicit instructions.

Such intelligence is a necessary and integral component that should help the conventional programs with capabilities of learning and adapt on their own. It is no secret that machine learning will continue to expand and influence virtually all spheres of our lives. With the ever-expanding volumes of data, there's a good reason why data analysis smart will become ubiquitous and an integral component of any technological system.

Chapter 2

Introduction to Statistics and Probability Theory

You may be wondering, "What is the relationship between probability theory and machine learning?"

Well, Machine learning is a broad field that intersects several other fields such as statistics and probability theory, AI and computer science algorithmic field that helps to build programs that can iteratively learn on their own and extract meaningful insights from large sets of data. To unlock the immense potential of machine learning in a given application, a thorough understanding of statistics and probability theory is necessary for a good grasp of machine learning to get the best intelligent systems.

Obviously, there are several reasons why statistical and probability theory is essential ingredients of machine learning. Some of these reasons are:

- Selecting the algorithm that provides the best balance of accuracy, number of parameters, training time, and model complexity;
- Selecting the appropriate parameter settings for the program and its validation strategies;
- Identifying the bias-variance tradeoffs that cause underfitting and over fitting; and
- Estimating the right confidence interval and level of uncertainty in the program's decisions.

Therefore, this chapter explores concepts of statistics and probability theory that are essential in machine learning.

Random variables

Random variables play a significant role in probability theory. In probability theory, a random variable, usually denoted as X, is a variable whose possible values are primarily numerical outcomes of a random experiment or phenomenon. Random variables can be either discrete or continuous, which means they are actually functions that can map outcomes to real values within the outcome space. Let me explain using the following example:

Suppose you throw a die. Let X represents the random variable that relies on the outcome of the throw. Obviously, the natural choice for X would be to map the outcome denoted as i to the value of i. An X outcome of 1, for instance, would map the event of throwing a one on the die to the value of 1. (We could also choose strange mappings such as a variable Y that maps all outcomes to 0, but that would be a tedious and boring function.) The probability (P) of outcome i of random variable X is denoted as either $P(X = i)$ or $PX(i)$; in this way, you can avoid the formal notation of event spaces by defining random variables that capture the appropriate events.

Distributions

Probability distribution is the probability of each outcome of a random variable. Consider the following example:

Let random variable X again represent the outcome space of the die throw. Assuming that the die isn't loaded, we would expect the probability distribution of X to be as follows:

```
PX(1) = PX(2) = ... = PX(6) = 1/6
```

While this example is similar to the previous one, it has a different meaning: probability distribution is defined by the spectrum of events, whereas the previous example is defined by the random variable.

In probability theory, P(X) usually denotes the probability distribution (P) of random variable X. A distribution can include multiple variables simultaneously, in which case it is called a joint distribution because the probability is determined jointly by all the variables that are involved.

For example, let X be a random variable defined as the outcome space of a die throw and Y be a random variable that indicates the outcome of a coin flip, assigning a value of 1 if the coin turns up heads and a value of 0 if it turns up tails. Assuming that both the coin and the die are fair, the joint probability distribution of X and Y would be as follows:

P	X=1	X=2	X=3	X=4	X=5	X=6
Y=0	1/12	1/12	1/12	1/12	1/12	1/12
Y=1	1/12	1/12	1/12	1/12	1/12	1/12

We would denote this joint distribution as P(X,Y) and the probability of X having an outcome of a and Y having an outcome of b as either P(X = a, Y = b) or PX,Y(a,b).

Conditional distributions

Using a conditional distribution, the distribution of a random variable when the value of another random variable is known, we can base the probability of an event on the given outcome of another event. The conditional probability of random variable X = a given that random variable Y = b is defined as follows:

P(X = a|Y = b) = P(X = a, Y = b)/P(Y = b)

For example, suppose we want to determine the probability of throwing a one on a fair die given that the number thrown is odd. Let X be a random variable indicating the number thrown on the die and Y be a random variable that assigns the value of 1 to the event of throwing an odd number. The probability of throwing a one can then be calculated as follows:

```
P(X = 1|Y = 1) = P(X = 1,Y = 1)/P(Y = 1)
= (1/6)/(1/2) = 1/3
```

Conditional distributions are an important tool for designing systems that can reason about uncertainty.

Independence

A random variable is independent of another random variable when the variable's distribution doesn't change in response to the value of the other variable. In machine learning, we can make assumptions about data based on independence. For instance, training samples i and j are assumed to be independent of an underlying space when the label of sample i is unaffected by the features of sample j. In formal notation, random variable X is independent of random variable Y only when

$$P(X) = P(X|Y)$$

The values of X and Y have been dropped because the
statement is true for all values of X and Y.

Mean, variance, and standard deviation in statistical distribution

Mean

Also known as the expected value or the first moment,
the mean (E) of the distribution for each outcome (a) of
random variable X is defined as follows:

$$E(X) = \sum [a \cdot P(X = a)]$$

For all values of a being, members of values of variable
X.

In other words, the mean of distribution can be given
by the formula below:

$$\mu = \sum [x \cdot P(x)]$$

Where μ is the mean of the distribution. Consider the example below:

For example, let X be a random variable representing the outcome of throwing a fair die. The expected value of X can then be calculated as follows:

```
E(X)  =  [(1·(1)¹/6)]  ₆  +  [(2·(1)¹/6)]  ₆  +
...· · · +  [(6·)(1 ¹ /6)]₆ = 3.5 ¹/ ₂
```

The mean of a random variable X is useful for assessing the expected of the variable's distribution. For instance, if you're a stockbroker, you may want to know the expected value of a client's investments in a year's time. You may be want to investigate the risk of your investment. In other words, how likely it is that the value of your investment will deviate from its expectation?

Variance

To protect the client from unacceptable financial
losses, the stockbroker may also want to estimate the
amount of risk involved in an investment by calculating
its variance. The variance or second moment of a
probability distribution is the degree of disparity within
the distribution, defined in formal notation as

$$\text{Var}(X) \;=\; E\,\{[X \,-\, E(X)]^2\}$$

where X is a random variable and E is the mean of the
distribution. However, variance is much easier to
compute using the following formula:

$$\text{Var}(X) \;=\; E(X^2) \;-\; [E(X)]^2$$

Instead of

$$\text{Var}(X) \;=\; E\,((X \,-\, E(X))^2)$$

Standard deviation

The variance of a random variable's distribution measures only the average degree of disparity, which is why its use is mostly confined to calculating risk. To more accurately determine how much the random variable deviates from its expected value, the standard deviation is used instead. The standard deviation (σ) of the distribution of random variable X is the square root of the distribution variance:

$$\sigma = \sqrt{\left[\sum [x^2 \cdot P(x)] - \mu^2 \right]}$$

Where σ is the standard deviation of the probability distribution.

Marginalization

Suppose the random variables X and Y comprise a joint distribution, P(X, Y), and we want to isolate the distribution of X, P(X); we can accomplish this either by summing out Y if X is a discrete random variable or by integrating Y if X is a continuous random variable.

Such an operation is called marginalization.

```
P(x; y)
```

This means that given the joint density, we can recover the `P(x)` by summing it out with y if it is a discrete random variable or integrating it with y if it is a continuous random variable. Such an operation is called marginalization.

Put simply, if X is a discrete random variable, then we can have the following distribution:

```
p(x) = Σ p(x; y)
```

For all values of y. In such a scenario, we say that the random variables X and Y are independent which mean that the values that X assumes don't depend on the values that Y assumes.

```
p(x; y) = p(x)p(y)
```

Independence is vital when you're dealing with large numbers of random variables whose behavior you want to estimate jointly. For example, whenever you do repeated measurements of a quantity such as measuring the voltages of a device, you can assume individual measurements and estimate the large sets of devices that you're dealing with.

On the other hand, dependence can be useful for classification and regression problems. For example, the traffic lights are dependent on each other at an intersection. If you're a driver, you can infer that when the lights are green in your direction, there won't be traffic crossing your path since the other lights will be red. Equally, whenever you are given a picture x of any digit, you hope that there will be some dependence between that picture and label y.

This can formally be represented as:

$$p(x \mid y) := p(x; y)/(p(y))$$

Bayes' theorem

Using the axioms of conditional probability, Bayes' theorem describes the process of updating the probabilities of hypotheses when new evidence is uncovered, but it can also be a powerful tool for reasoning about a broad range of problems that

involve belief updates. Given two events, E and H,
Bayes' theorem is defined in formal notation as
follows:

$$P(H|E) \ = \ \frac{P(H) \cdot P(E|H)}{P(E)}$$

The applications of Bayes' theorem have produced a
new field of probability theory called Bayesian
statistics, revolutionizing scientific research but also
medicine, law, quality analysis, and every other
discipline that draws inferences from uncertain
evidence.

Chapter 3

Building Blocks of Machine Learning

Machine-learning algorithms have attracted more interest than ever before, generating a flood of innovative ideas for applications of this technology. For tech enthusiasts interested in developing machine-learning programs, the greatest challenge is about understanding the fundamental concepts involved in these projects.

In this chapter, we explore the building blocks of machine learning that will help you close the gap. By the end of the chapter, you should be in a position to understand the finite elements of machine learning that can help you turn ideas into hardware and software primitives.

Formal statistical learning frameworks

Statistical learning contexts can simplify learning processes in computers. Allow me to illustrate using an example.

Suppose you've landed on an island where the natives love to eat papaya, a fruit with which you are unfamiliar. You're standing in the marketplace, trying to figure out which papayas are the best. Based on your previous experiences with fresh fruit, you decide to examine the color and softness of each papaya. The colors range from red to dark brown, while the softness ranges from rock solid to mushy; in statistical terms, these are two sets of inputs to help you predict the taste of each papaya.

Let us now construct a model to describe this learning process, which is called a formal statistical learning framework. The model must incorporate the following components:

- Learner's input
- Learner's output
- Simple data-generalization model
- Measures of success

Let's examine each of these critical elements.

#1: Learner's input

- **The domain set.** The domain is an arbitrary set containing the objects, also called points, to be labeled. In this case, the domain set is the set of all papayas. Domain points can be represented using vectors of features such as a papaya's color and softness.
- **The label set**. The label set contains the predictions made about the domain points. For this scenario, the label set can be restricted to a two-element set where Y represents the papayas you think will taste good and X represents the papayas you think will taste bad.

- ***The training data***. The training data is a set containing `((x1; y1):::` `(xm; ym))` that has a finite sequence of pairs in the $X \times Y$ matrix that are accessed to test the accuracy of the label set. In this example, the training data is the set of papayas you buy so you can find out how they taste.

#2: Learner's output

The output is the creation of the prediction rule, also called the predictor, hypothesis, or classifier, used to label the domain points. In this example, the prediction rule is the standard you use to decide whether you think a papaya will taste good or bad. Prediction rules are typically based on previous experiences.

#3: Data-generalization model

The data-generalization model uses a function to generate the training data based on the probability distribution of the domain set. In this case, the data-generalization model is the method by which you choose a representative sample of papayas to buy. However, the learner might not always know what the distribution is, so the model's design must ensure that the labels apply to any probability distribution. For instance, the function can take either of the following forms:

```
f : X ! Y
```

or

```
Yᵢ yi= f(Xᵢxi)
```

for all values of i.

```
Such a function can now be used to
generate the training data that the
learner will now use.
```

#4: Measures of success

Obviously, there must be a way to calculate the training error or error of the predictor, the probability that the statistical learning framework incorrectly predicts the outcomes of the learning process and thus fails to meet the desired objectives. Since the objective of this scenario is to select the best papayas, the error of the predictor can be determined by conducting a taste test of the papayas you bought to find out whether they're as good or bad as you expected them to be.

Empirical risk

In the situation sometimes called agnostic learning, a machine-learning algorithm receives input from a training set that is sampled from an unknown distribution. The goal of the machine-learning algorithm is to minimize error, but since the learner doesn't know what the distribution is, the exact computational error cannot be determined.

Any useful notion of the error that can be computed by the learner will be the training error, which is the error that the classifier gets from the training sample.

In summary, the minimization risk $R(h)$ can't be computed since the distribution D is unidentified to the machine- learning program under such circumstances— a situation that is sometimes called agnostic learning— and the function is minimized. However, we can use an approximation which is the empirical risk. Every learning model has a loss function that measures the degree of inaccuracy in the model's predictions. To calculate the empirical risk, the smallest values in the training set are plugged into the loss function, which is called minimizing or leveraging the function.

PAC learning strategies

In the previous sections, we have seen how a finite hypothesis class and the training data set rule can be applied to train a computer on how to adapt to certain tasks whose size is independent on the underlying distribution D and the unknown function f. However, we haven't defined the role of "Probably Approximately Correct" (PAC) learning.

At the core of probably approximately correct (PAC) learning are two approximation parameters: First, the accuracy parameter and the second is the output classifier.

- The accuracy parameter determines how often the output classifier can make a correct prediction.
- The confidence parameter measures the probability that the predictor will attain this level of accuracy.

Although PAC learning can be useful even when a model's training data accurately represent the distribution, it is especially vital for handling the inevitable uncertainties of the data-access model. This model always generates random training sets with a small chance of producing an uninformative training set that has only one domain point.

Generalization models for machine learning

The data-access model that we have discussed in the previous section can readily be use to represent the wider scope of learning processes in general. By generalization, we mean having two essential components:

- Removing the reliability assumption
- Revisiting the true error rate

When the reliability assumption has been met, we can expect a machine-learning algorithm to generate training data that reliably reflect the distribution. However, such an assumption can be impractical, placing unrealistic standards on the algorithm.

Moreover, a learning algorithm is never guaranteed to find a hypothesis with the best possible error rate like that of the Bayes predictor. Once we make no previous assumptions about data-generating distribution, there is no algorithm will guarantee the production of predictors that are as good as the Bayes optimal one.

Instead, it is reasonable to expect the algorithm to find a predictor whose error rate isn't much less than optimal.

Chapter 4

Basic Machine-Learning Algorithms

This chapter explores some problems commonly encountered by machine-learning programs in various applications and introduces the types of algorithms that are used to solve these problems.

Challenges of machine learning

The predominant theme of all machine-learning problems is finding relationships between sets of data. However, the specific problem that machine learning seeks to solve depends on the application, so the following synopses briefly describe typical program designs for some common applications and the challenges inherent in these designs:

1. Search engines.

   Probably the most familiar application of machine learning, search engines are designed to find the Web pages that are most relevant to a user's query. To accomplish this goal, a search engine needs to figure out which pages are relevant and which ones exactly match the query. The program can draw its conclusions from a variety of inputs, such as the words in each link, the content of each page, or how frequently users follow the suggested links.

2. Collaborative filtering.

   Collaborative filtering is the learning process by which online retailers such as Amazon recommend items that customers may be interested in buying. These programs are similar to search engines, but relevancy is based on trends in a user's past purchases rather than on direct input from the user.

3. Automatic translation.

A particularly challenging task in machine learning is automatic translation of documents. It's one thing for a computational linguist to develop a curated set of rules for a program to follow, but it's quite another for the program to understand the words in a document and learn other rules of syntax and grammar on its own, especially since documents aren't always grammatically correct. One solution is to design a program that learns how to translate languages by using examples of translated documents.

4. Named identity recognition.

The challenge of identifying entities such as places, titles, actions and names from documents can easily be modeled and developed in machine learning systems. These tasks are vital in the automatic digestion and comprehension of documents. For instance, modern email clients such as the Google's Gmail and Apple's Mail are nowadays being shipped with the ability to identify email addresses in them and filling them in address the phone's address book.

While machine-learning systems that use handcrafted rules can produce satisfactory results, it is far more effective to use examples of other marked-up documents to learn from such dependencies automatically so that the machine learning system is efficient in named identity recognition.

5. Speech recognition

The predominant theme of all machine-learning problems is that there exists a nontrivial dependence between some observations that we commonly refer to as x and the desired response that we commonly refer to as y for which set of rules are not known. By using machine learning, we can infer some of these dependencies between x and y using algorithms that can associate between these two sets of data.

For instance, we can annotate any audio sequence with the text data such as Apple's Siri, the recognition of handwriting and signatures and the avatar behavior that is used in computer games. This information had increasingly led to the development of robotic systems that are far much more efficient in work than when these systems were not there.

6. Facial recognition.

These days, facial recognition is a primary component of many security and access-control systems. Using photos or video recordings, such a system is designed to allow only people it recognizes into the building or information system it's guarding. The difficult part, of course, is verifying a person's identity; a machine-learning program is far more effective in this regard, since a system that learns from its mistakes is much harder to fool than one with a rigid set of standards.

Types of learning

Machine learning is a broad field with several different subfields of learning processes. These subfields can be grouped into three main categories based on their goals:

- Supervised learning
- Unsupervised learning
- Reinforcement learning

Let's explore these types of machine learning.

#1: Supervised learning

Supervised learning takes place when an algorithm learns to correctly predict responses to input data by using examples and their associated target responses. The target responses can range from numerical values to string labels such as tags. This learning process is like a teacher giving examples to students in a class, who then memorize these examples and extract general rules from them. Examples of these learning algorithms include the following:

- Decision trees
- Random forest

- KNN
- Regression algorithms

Chapter 5 discusses these algorithms in greater detail.

#2: Unsupervised learning

As the name suggests, unsupervised learning takes place when an algorithm learns from examples without any associated responses. In other words, the algorithm is left to determine its own data patterns from the given set of inputs. This type of algorithm usually restructures the data into classes or even a new series of uncorrelated values, kind of like a person creating categories of similar objects or events. Unsupervised learning is quite useful for discovering new insights from large sets of data and generating new inputs for supervised machine-learning algorithms. Examples of unsupervised learning algorithms include the following:

- Clustering algorithm
- Markov algorithm
- Neural networks

These algorithms are further discussed in Chapter 6.

#3: Reinforcement learning

Reinforcement learning is like unsupervised learning except with input that is accompanied by positive or negative feedback mechanisms depending on how the algorithm works. Essentially the equivalent of trial and error, this type of learning is useful for applications that require the algorithm to make its own decisions based on the consequences of its actions, seeking good outcomes while trying to avoid mistakes. A perfect example of such an application is Google's DeepMind program that plays Atari games. The following are typical reinforcement machine-learning algorithms:

- Q-learning
- SARSA

Chapter 7 focuses on these algorithms.

Chapter 5

Supervised Machine-Learning Algorithms

As we had discussed earlier, supervised learning algorithms are those algorithms that consist of a target and outcome variable which is to be forecasted from a given set of predictors that forms the independent variables. By using these sets of variables, you can produce a function that maps the inputs to desired outputs. Such a training process continues until the machine-learning model achieves its desired level of accuracy on the training data.

Decision Trees, Regression, Random Forest, KNN and Logistic Regression are some examples of supervised learning algorithms. We are going to understand and learn more about them. This chapter delves deeper into the mechanics behind the main types of supervised machine-learning algorithms. Let's jump in.

Decision trees

Decision trees are excellent, highly efficient data-analysis tools that can help you choose one alternative from several alternative actions. They provide a highly efficient structure that allow you to lay out options and examine the possible outcomes of each option, providing you with a balanced picture of all their pros and cons. Surprisingly, these algorithms work for both categorical and continuous random variables, though they are mostly used to solve classification problems. A decision tree splits the entire domain set into two or more sets of similar data, sorting them by independent variables that distinguish the sets. Let me illustrate using an example.

Suppose you have a sample of 60 students that has three independent variables: gender (Boy/Girl), class

(IY/Y), and height (5 to 6 feet). You know that 30 of these students play soccer in their free time, and you want to design a model that can figure out the identity of each soccer player. To solve this problem, a decision tree divides the sample into groups based on the three variables, seeking to create homogeneous sets of students.

Decision trees use one of several algorithms to help them split a given set into two or more subsets, producing increasingly homogeneous outcomes; the exact algorithm chosen depends on the types of variables involved. The following algorithms are among the most commonly used:

- **The Gini index.** The Gini index works as follows: If two items with the same value of a target variable are randomly selected, then they must be in the same class and probability. The categorical value of the target variable is marked by another variable as either success or failure, which the algorithm converts into a binary split within the class. The Gini scores of the subclasses are then calculated as the squares of their respective probabilities within the class and added together to determine the Gini index of the class. The higher a class's Gini index, the greater its homogeneity.

- The higher the value of the Gini index, the greater the homogeneity.

  For the sub-nodes, we compute the Gini index that is denoted as the square of probability for success and failure using the formula: (p^2+q^2). Compute the Gini for the split using the weighted Gini score of each node of the split.

- *Chi-square.* The chi-square algorithm is used to find out whether any significant statistical differences exist between sets and their respective subsets. The degree of statistical significance is measured by summing the squares of standardized differences between the observed and expected frequencies of the target variable.

- *Reduction in variance.* Reduction in variance is used for continuous target variables. The algorithm selects the splits with the lowest variances among the variables.

Advantages of decision trees

- A decision tree's output is easy to understand even if you don't have any statistical training.

- The decision-tree algorithm is one of the fastest ways to identify the most significant variables and the relationships between them, making it ideal for data exploration.

- Compared to other learning models, the algorithm doesn't require a lot of data cleaning.

- The algorithm can handle both numerical and categorical variables.

Disadvantages of decision trees

- Decision trees tend to overfit data, so they require many variable constraints that are tedious to design.

- The algorithm is ill suited for continuous variables because it loses information during the categorization of variables.

Random forest

Every data scientist uses the random-forest algorithm at some point, which is why this algorithm is considered to be the panacea for all data-science problems. A versatile machine-learning algorithm that combines several techniques into one robust model, random forest can perform regression, classification, and dimensional-reduction tasks, as well as handle essential data-exploration tasks such as treating outliers and missing values. The random-forest algorithm consists of multiple decision trees that classify each object in the training set; using a process that resembles voting, the forest selects the classification chosen by the majority of the trees. Here's how the algorithm works:

- Every object in the training set is randomly generated and can be replaced as necessary.
- If there are M input variables, then a number $m<M$ is specified and held constant so that each tree can select m variables at random from M.
- Each tree finds the best split for m.
- All the trees grow to the largest extent possible without pruning.
- The forest then predicts the outcome by aggregating all the trees' predictions and selecting either the majority consensus for classification or the average for regression.

Let's look at an illustration of the random-forest algorithm in action. Note that the figures quoted in this book are for illustrative purposes only.

Suppose the algorithm's training set contains socioeconomic data about 10,000 Kenyans out of the total population of 40,000,000 people. For the sake of simplicity, let the model be built on 1 target variable, salary bands in Kenyan shillings (Ksh.). In total, 5 different decision trees are built using 3 other variables: age, gender, and level of education. Here are the categorical values of the target variable: Suppose we select salary as our variable for the development of the model; then we have the following scenarios:

Salary Bands

Band 1: Below Ksh. 20,000

Band 2: Ksh. 20,000 to Ksh. 100,000

Band 3: Above Ksh. 100,000

The above salary bands are then split based on the 3 variables:

 Variable: Age

Age	Band 1	Band 2	Band 3
Below 18 years	90%	50%	40%
18 to 27 years	75%	43%	28%
28 to 40 years	51%	30%	16%
Above 40 years	34%	22%	10%

Variable: Gender

Gender	Band 1	Band 2	Band 3
Male	71%	47%	70%
Female	83%	60%	45%

Variable: Level of education

Education	Band 1	Band 2	Band 3
College certificate	90%	50%	40%
College diploma	75%	43%	28%
College degree	51%	30%	16%
Master's and above	34%	22%	10%

Using the above aggregate data, the algorithm now builds a single mean probabilistic model to predict the salary band of one of the training data that can map the above data into a single probabilistic model, For simplicity, we can use the mean probabilistic model to develop the unique framework for modeling the above information. Let's say a 30-year-old Kenyan male who has a college degree, which produces the following result:

Variable	Input	Band 1	Band 2	Band 3
Age	28 to 40 years	51%	30%	16%
Gender	Male	71%	47%	70%
Education	College degree	51%	30%	16%

Advantages of random forest

- The random-forest algorithm can solve both classification and regression problems.
- Random forest can handle colossal sets of data and thousands of input variables with higher dimensionality.
- The algorithm can estimate missing data with a sufficient level of accuracy.
- The algorithm can correct imbalances in the error rate between datasets.

Disadvantages of random forest

- In regression problems, random forest doesn't predict beyond the ranges that are given in the training data, so its results may not be as accurate as those of other algorithms.

- You have little control over what the algorithm does, so you can only assume that it gives you the output you want.

KNN algorithm

The k-nearest neighbors (KNN) algorithm searches the entire training dataset for the k most similar examples of a certain data instance, then summarizes the results and uses them to predict the attributes of that instance.

The model is also competitive learning in the sense that it internally uses competition between the model elements—the data instances—to make a predictive decision. The overarching objective is to measure the similarities between data instances that provide the hidden data instance that is necessary for making predictions.

A lazy learning process, the algorithm doesn't build a model until it is asked for a prediction, which keeps the data relevant to the task at hand. Let's look at a practical example to demonstrate how the model works.

Suppose we have 150 observations of flowers from 3 different species: *Iris setosa*, *I. versicolor*, and *I. virginica*. The algorithm's objective is to predict the species of a flower based on 4 measurements: sepal length, sepal width, petal length, and petal width. To identify the species of flower, the algorithm selects the training set and computes the distance between any two data instances, basing its prediction on the flower's k closest resemblances. We can assume that good classification accuracy is at least above 90% correct.

Here's the summary of how the classification will be done:

Generate the input data. The input data forms part of the training data. In the flower example, we have 150 observations of the iris flowers from 3 different species that have different sepal lengths, sepal widths, petal lengths and the petal widths.

Compute the distance between any two data instances (determine the kth nearest neighbor) to determine the similarity levels.

Locate the k most similar among the neighbors.

Generate a response based on the data instances.

Summarize the accuracy of the predictions.

Advantages of the KNN algorithm

- The KNN algorithm cuts through noise in the training set as its competitive, instance-based model seeks only the data with the most desired attributes.
- Like random forest, the KNN algorithm can easily handle large datasets and thousands of input variables with high levels of dimensionality.

Disadvantages of the KNN algorithm

- Since the algorithm analyzes all the training data before making a prediction, its computational cost is high compared to other machine-learning algorithms.
- Like decision trees, the KNN algorithm often overfits data, so it too requires many variable constraints that are tedious to design.
- The algorithm is unsuitable for continuous variables.

Regression algorithms

Regression analysis investigates relationships between dependent or target variables and independent or predictor variables. This technique is used for forecasting, time-series modeling, and finding causal relationships between variables such as reckless driving and number of traffic accidents. These algorithms are designed to fit a curve or line to the data points as closely as possible. Let's look at an example illustrating how these algorithms are used.

Suppose you want to estimate the sales growth in your company based on current economic conditions. Using your company's past and current performance data, a regression algorithm shows you the growth trend. If you know that your company is growing about twice as fast as the overall economy, for instance, you can predict future sales growth.

There are various types of regression algorithms, among which the following are the most common:

- Linear regression
- Logistic regression
- Polynomial regression

- Stepwise regression
- Ridge regression

Let us now examine some of the properties of these regression algorithms.

#1: Linear regression algorithm

One of the simplest and most widely used regression algorithms, this technique establishes a best-fit linear relationship between a dependent variable (Y), which is usually continuous, and an independent variable (X), which can be either continuous or discrete. When Y is plotted against X on a Cartesian plane, the regression line is generated using the equation

```
Y = a + (b·*X) + e
```

where a is the Y intercept and b is the slope of the line. The line is then used to predict the value of the target variable based on the given predictor variable.

#2: Logistic regression algorithm

An ideal algorithm for classification problems, logistic regression is used to determine the probability of the outcome (success or failure) of a binary dependent variable (e.g. 0 or 1, true or false, yes or no). In this form of regression, the probability ranges from 0 to 1 and is calculated using one of the equations

```
odds = p/(1-p)
ln(odds) = ln[p/(1-p)]
logit(p) = ln[p/(1-p)] = b₀ + b₁X₁ + b₂X₂ +
b₃X₃ + ... + bₖXₖ
```

where p is the probability of a particular outcome of the dependent variable, x is the independent variable, and b is the best-fit parameter.

#3: Polynomial Regression Algorithm

As the name suggests, a polynomial- regression algorithm generates a polynomial when the dependent variable (Y) is plotted against an independent variable (x), whose power is greater than 1, on a Cartesian plane. The polynomial is a best-fit curve represented by the equation

```
Y = a + (b·X²)
```

where a is the Y intercept and b is the best-fit parameter.

#4: Stepwise Regression algorithm

Stepwise regression is used when dealing with multiple independent variables. In this regression technique, the independent variables are automatically selected based on statistical values such as R-squared, t-statistics, and the Akaike information criterion. The model then fits the regression data by adding and dropping the covariates one at a time in accordance with a specified criterion, which can be among the following most common approaches:

- Standard stepwise regression simply adds or removes predictors as needed for each step of regression.
- Forward selection begins with the most significant predictor and adds one variable at each level in the model.
- Backward elimination starts with all the predictors in the model and removes the least significant variable at each stage.

#5: Ridge Regression

Ridge regression is used when a dataset suffers from multicollinearity, in which independent variables are so highly correlated that their variances may deviate from their observed values even though the model's ordinary-least-squares estimates are unbiased. By adding a given degree of bias to the estimates, ridge regression reduces standard errors. If the model is a linear regression, for example, the equation

```
Y = a + (b·X)
```

has an error term (e) added to become

```
Y = a + (b·X) + e
```

Factors to consider when selecting a regression-analysis technique

Below are some useful factors that you should consider when choosing a particular regression analysis method:

- How do you want to explore your data? Data exploration is an unavoidable component of developing a predictive model and therefore should be one of the initial considerations in selecting the right technique.

- Which statistical metrics do you want to include in your learning algorithm? You may be interested in several metrics such as the statistical significance of the parameters, R-squared, adjusted R-squared, and the error term, in which case stepwise regression may be the best technique for your purposes.

- How do you want to evaluate the predictive model? Cross-validation is the best approach to assessing the model; a simple mean squared deviation between the observed and the predicted values gives you a good idea of the prediction accuracy.
- Does the dataset have multiple independent variables? If these variables can confound the model, then you should avoid the automatic selection method so you don't have to use all the variables simultaneously.

Advantages of regression algorithms

- Regression algorithms show significant relationships between dependent variables and independent variables.
- The algorithms show the impact of multiple independent variables on a dependent variable.
- You can compare the effects of independent variables that are measured differently, such as the impact of price changes and promotional activities.

Disadvantages of regression algorithms

- Regression algorithms can't be applied to classification problems.

The algorithms have a tendency to overfit data, so you need to incorporate many variable constraints, a tedious process.

Chapter 6

Unsupervised Machine Learning Algorithms

In this chapter, we explore the ins and outs of unsupervised machine-learning algorithms.

Clustering algorithm

The clustering algorithm is a simple way to classify any given dataset using a particular number of clusters that are then divided into homogeneous subgroups. Here's how clustering works:

- The algorithm selects the number of points for each main cluster. For the sake of clarity, let these clusters be called centroids.
- Each data point clusters with the centroid with which it shares the most attributes.
- Each centroid is then divided into more clusters based on similarities between its members.
- With each new set of clusters within a centroid, further division occurs until the centroids no longer change, which is called convergence.

The sum of the squares of the differences between data points within a cluster and those in the rest of their centroid constitutes the value for that cluster. Likewise, the total value of the centroids is the sum of the squared values for all the clusters.

Advantages of the clustering algorithm

- The clustering algorithm's computational cost is low compared to other machine-learning algorithms.
- The algorithm is a very efficient classification system.

Disadvantages of the clustering algorithm

- The clustering algorithm may not work for prediction problems.
- If its centroids are improperly categorized, then the entire clustering algorithm may not produce the desired results.

Markov algorithm

The Markov algorithm uses a predetermined set of rules to translate a string of input data into another language, which makes it useful for finding parameters that dictate the behavior of a dataset with a known range of values. For instance, the algorithm can convert DNA sequences into numerical outputs that are easier to analyze for underlying patterns.

Advantages of the Markov algorithm

- The algorithm is ideal for learning problems with known inputs but unspecified parameters.
- The model can reveal hidden insights that other models can't detect.

Disadvantage of the Markov algorithm

- The model requires you to create a different set of rules for each programing language.

Neural networks

Neural networks analyze and learn patterns through various layers of neurons. Each layer looks for patterns in an image; if a pattern is detected, the next layer is activated, and the process repeats itself until the network is ready to predict what object the image portrays. If the prediction is correct, the neurons strengthen their association between the patterns and the object. Allow me to illustrate using an example.

Suppose you design a program that learns to recognize models of cars by various features such as the car's color and license plate. When you show an image of a car to the neural network, the first layer of the system detects the edges of the car, then the following layers each try to identify a specific characteristic, ultimately factoring in small details such as wheel patterns or even window patterns. The more features the neural network identifies, the more accurate its prediction tends to be. If the neural network successfully identifies the car's model, it learns to associate these patterns with this particular model so that they become easier to recognize with each successive encounter.

72

Advantages of neural networks

- Understanding neural networks doesn't require much formal statistical training.

- The algorithms can implicitly detect complex nonlinear relationships between dependent variables and independent variables.

- The algorithms can identify all the possible interactions between predictor variables and target variables.

Disadvantages of neural networks

- Neural networks have high computational costs.

The algorithms may not correctly analyze relationships between target variables and predictor variables.

Chapter 7

Reinforcement Machine Learning Algorithms

Since reinforcement learners don't require any expert supervision, the types of problems that they are best suited for are usually complex. Examples of these problems include the following:

- **Game playing.** When playing a game, the learner finds the best move based on various factors and the number of possible states in the game. Reinforcement learning eliminates the need for manually specifying all the rules.

- **Control problems.** Unlike both supervised and unsupervised learning, reinforcement learning can develop management policies for complex issues such as elevator scheduling.

Two approaches can be employed in reinforcement learning:

- **Indirect learning.** Indirect learning estimates an explicit model of the environment and then computes its optimal policy for the estimated model.
- **Direct learning.** In the direct-learning approach, the optimal policy is learned even without first learning the particular model.

Now that you know the basic strategies of reinforcement learning, let's explore two of the most common algorithms.

Q-learning

Often used for temporal-difference learning, Q-learning is an off-policy algorithm that learns an action-value function to provide the expected utility of taking a given action in a particular state. Since the algorithm can use any such function, the policy rule must specify how the learner selects a course of action.

Once the action-value function has been determined, the optimal policy can be constructed using the actions that have the highest values in each of the states. One advantage of Q-learning is that it doesn't need a model of the environment to compare the expected utility of all the available actions. The algorithm also doesn't have to adapt to problems with stochastic transitions and rewards.

SARSA

State-action-reward-state-action (SARSA) is an algorithm that describes a Markov decision-process policy where the main function for updating the q-value relies on the current state of the learner, the action that the learner chooses, the reward that the learner gets for selecting the action, and the state that the learner will be in after taking the action. Since the SARSA algorithm learns the safest path to the solution, it receives a higher average reward for any trial than the Q-learning algorithm does, even though it doesn't choose the optimal path.

CONCLUSION

From search engines to facial-recognition systems to driverless cars, machine learning is revolutionizing the once-dull AI field of IT. Smart programmers stay ahead of the curve by staying well informed about the latest technological advances, and now you have all the basic tools you need to join the revolution and start designing machine-learning programs yourself.

FURTHER RESOURCES

1. https://www.sas.com/en_us/insights/analytics/machine-learning.html
2. http://www.kdnuggets.com/2016/08/10-algorithms-machine-learning-engineers.html
3. http://cdn.intechopen.com/pdfs/10694.pdf
4. http://disp.ee.ntu.edu.tw/~pujols/Machine%20Learning%20Tutorial.pdf
5. http://mlss08.rsise.anu.edu.au/files/smola.pdf
6. http://www.ulb.ac.be/di/map/gbonte/mod_stoch/syl.pdf
7. http://scribd-download.com/essentials-of-machine-learning-algorithms-with-python-and-r-codes_58a2f7506454a7a940b1e8ec_pdf.html
8. http://machinelearningmastery.com/supervised-and-unsupervised-machine-learning-algorithms/
9. https://www.saylor.org/site/wp-content/uploads/2011/11/CS405-6.2.1.2-WIKIPEDIA.pdf
10. https://page.mi.fu-berlin.de/rojas/neural/chapter/K5.pdf

11. http://www.cs.upc.edu/~bejar/apren/docum/trans/09-clusterej-eng.pdf

12. http://webee.technion.ac.il/people/shimkin/LCS11/ch4_RL1.pdf

13. http://web.mst.edu/~gosavia/neural_networks_RL.pdf

ABOUT THE AUTHOR

Matt Gates is an associate university lecturer with more than 10 years of teaching experience on academic subjects ranging from IT management, software development, and machine learning to data modeling. He believes that the next phase of IT development lies in AI, Machine Learning and Automation.

Matt hopes to use his books to share his knowledge to impact thousands of people.

In his spare time, Matt often engage in discussions on Reddit, forums and buy the latest gadgets on Amazon.

Matt's Message

Thank you for reading! This book is a starter quick guide on Machine Learning to help you familiarize with the basic understanding on what is Machine Learning and the various type of algorithms (including their pros and cons) that are available for your further exploration.

If you would like to read more great books like this one, why not subscribe to our website.

https://www.auvapress.com/vip

Thanks for reading! Please add your short review on Amazon

and let me know what your thoughts! – Matt

Other Victor's Titles You Will Find Useful

Blockchain Technology

Blockchain is a revolution that you should not ignore anymore.

Imagine you are been presented with an opportunity before the flourishing of Internet, what would you do? Now is the time!

BLOCKCHAIN TECHNOLOGY

THE ESSENTIAL QUICK & EASY BLUEPRINT TO
UNDERSTAND BLOCKCHAIN TECHNOLOGY AND
CONQUER THE NEXT THRIVING ECONOMY!
GET YOUR FIRST MOVER ADVANTAGE NOW!

—— VICTOR FINCH ——

- You will understand everything you need to know about the mechanics of Blockchain.
- You will learn how you can benefit from Blockchain
- You will learn the legal implications of Blockchain technology

Victor Finch
ISBN: 978-1-5413-6684-8
Paperback: 102 Pages
eBook, Audiobook Available

Bitcoin

Are you still wondering or clueless about
what is Bitcoin? Do you know Bitcoin is
thriving robustly as a digital currency
because of its characteristics for more
than 8 years.

You will understand everything (including
merits & demerits) you need to know
about Bitcoin
You will learn how to use Bitcoin and read
the transactions.
You will learn discover the best practices
in using Bitcoin securely.

Victor Finch
ISBN: 978-1-5441-4139-8
Paperback: 98 Pages
eBook, Audiobook Available

Other Auva Press Titles You Will Find Useful

Smart Contracts

Smart Contract is about the revolutionary (Blockchain Technology) approach with legal contracts or any legal agreements. This book offers an unprecedented peek into what the future may be like that could possibly change and enhance the traditional way of doing things for the better (many benefits).

- You will learn how disruptive (positive) are Smart Contracts
- You will learn about the legal perspectives of Smart Contracts.
- BONUS Highlight: More than 7 Possible Smart Contract Use Cases in different industries.

Victor Finch
ISBN: 978-1-5446-9150-3
Paperback: 106 Pages
eBook, Audiobook Available

Python

Python is a highly sought after skillset by many corporations. Possibilities with Python are limitless and often prefer over Java and C++ due to three characteristics that you will discover in this book.

- You will learn how to set up your first python.
- You will learn how to properly do error handling and debug to save you hours of time.
- **BONUSES** Included (plus Hands On Challenges)

Ronald Olsen
ISBN: 978-1-5426-6789-0
Paperback: 152 Pages
eBook, Audiobook Available

AUVA PRESS

AUVA Press commits lots of effort in the content research, planning and production of quality books. Every book is created with you in mind and you will receive the best possible valuable information in clarity and accomplish your goals.

If you like what you have seen and benefited from this helpful book, we would appreciate your honest review on Amazon or on your favorite social media.

Your review is appreciated and will go a long way to motivate us in producing more quality books for your reading pleasure and needs.

Visit Us Online

AUVA PRESS Books
https://www.auvapress.com/books

Register for Updates
https://www.auvapress.com/vip

Contact Us

AUVA Press books may be purchased in bulk for corporate, academic, gifts or promotional use.

For information on translation, licenses, media requests, please visit our contact page.
https://www.auvapress.com/contact

- END -

Made in the USA
Middletown, DE
30 June 2017